# Brain-TINGLING Mazes

## Patrick Merrell

STERLING PUBLISHING CO., INC.
New York

2  4  6  8  10  9  7  5  3  1

Published by Sterling Publishing Co., Inc.
387 Park Avenue South, New York, NY 10016
© 2005 by Patrick Merrell
Distributed in Canada by Sterling Publishing
$^c$/o Canadian Manda Group, 165 Dufferin Street
Toronto, Ontario, Canada M6K 3H6
Distributed in Great Britain and Europe by Chris Lloyd at Orca Book
Services, Stanley House, Fleets Lane, Poole BH15 3AJ, England
Distributed in Australia by Capricorn Link (Australia) Pty. Ltd.
P.O. Box 704, Windsor, NSW 2756, Australia

*Printed in China*

Sterling ISBN 1-4027-1877-2

# Contents

# Atta Buoy!

Here's a good maze to get your feet wet. Can you find the path of buoys from "Start" to "End"?

End

Start

# Bar Made

This pile of magnets is very attractive, isn't it? Can you find the path through it?

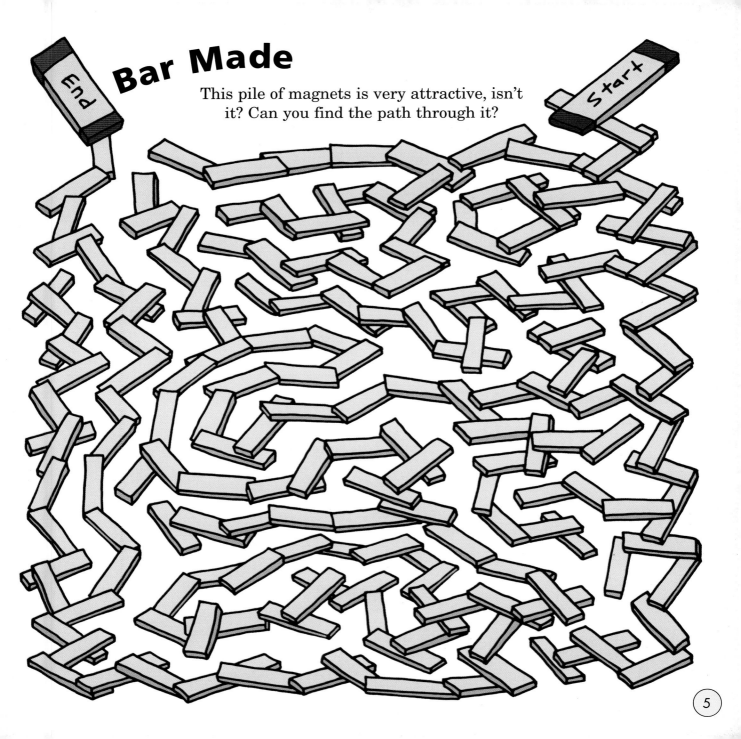

# Bear With It

This circus bear needs to find a route that crosses each one of these 10 spots exactly once. Can you help him?

Start

End!

# Brush Up

Pick the purple paint path that will propel you to the end.

# Can You Dig It?

Ever feel like you're stuck in a rut?
Hopefully that won't be the case with this maze.

**End**

**Start**

# Crayon Playing

You've got to think outside the box with this one!

# Crazy Mazy

Here's a crazy challenge for you. Good luck!

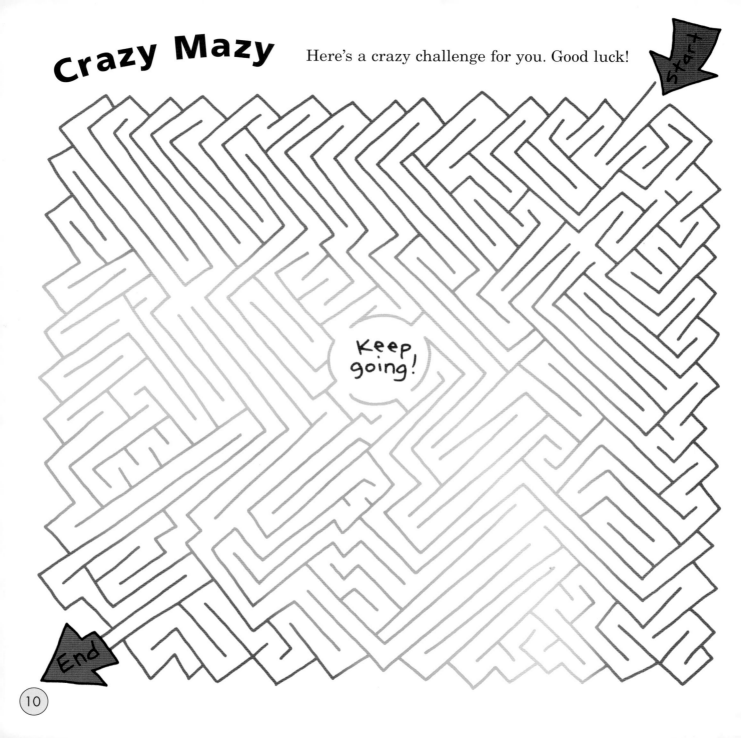

Start

Keep going!

End

# Crepe Race

Will you stroll or streak or struggle through this mess of streamers?

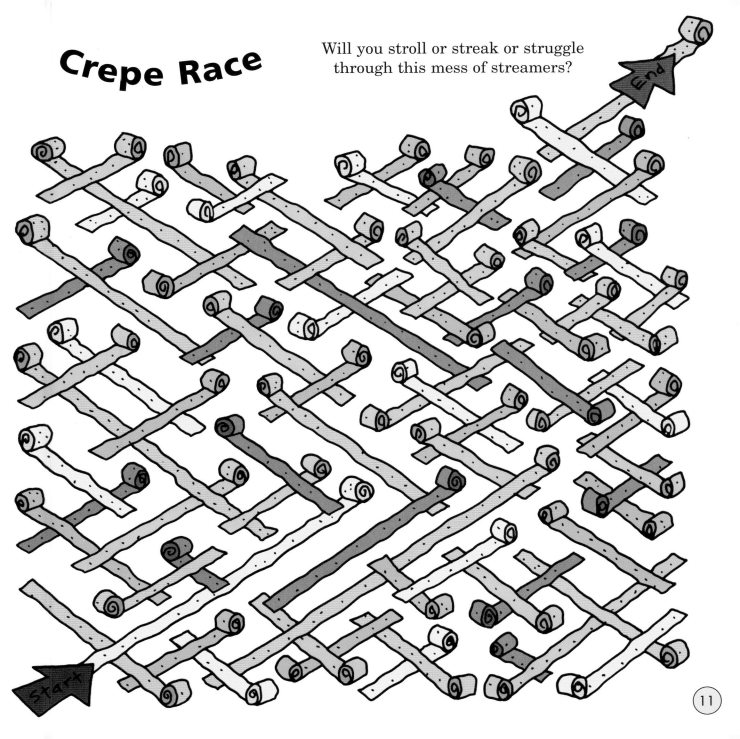

# Crowing Time

Go from the mouse to either the woodchuck or skunk. Either of those can go to two others, and so on. Keep going until you get to the chicken!

**Mouse** — Woodchuck · Skunk

**Skunk** — Frog · Woodchuck

**Fish** — Snake · Mouse

**Chick** — Fish · Bear

**Chicken**

**Woodchuck** — Fish · Snake

**Snake** — Mouse · Fish

**Frog** — Fish · Cow

**Platypus** — Chick · Mouse

**Ferret** — Fish · Chicken

**Raccoon** — Goose · Cat

**Cow** — Hippo · Snake

**Pig** — Raccoon · Goose

**Dog** — Ferret · Tiger

**Tiger** — Bat · Platypus

**Cat** — Pig · Raccoon

**Goose** — Cat · Pig

**Hippo** — Raccoon · Dog

**Bat** — Platypus · Tiger

**Bear** — Tiger · Bat

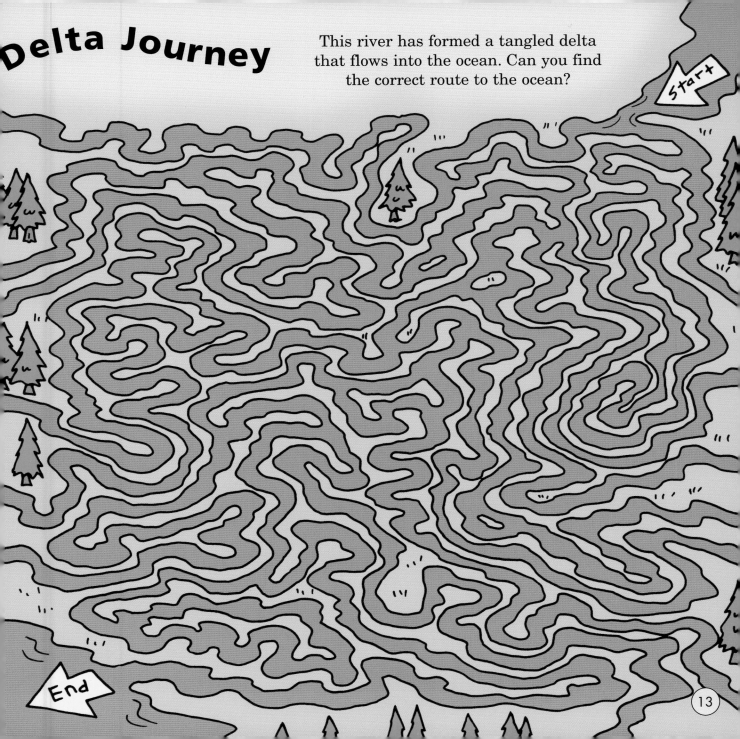

# Dot to Dot

**start**

**End**

Follow the arrows from dot to dot to dot to try to get to the end. Dots all there is to it!

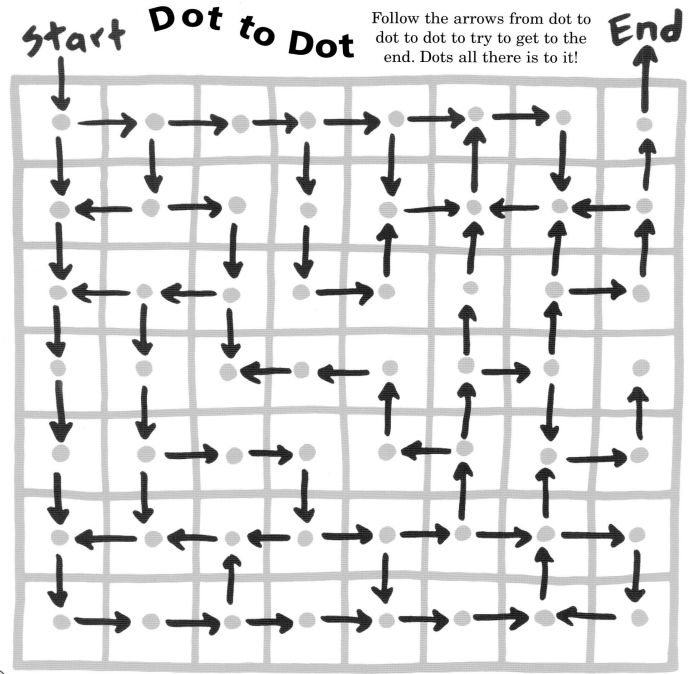

# Drawing the Line

Shar*pen* your wits and *open* your mind, and you'll be amazed at what will hap*pen* with this maze.

End

Start

15

# Easel Does It

An abstract work of art? No, just another maze that's fit for framing.

# Eggs-Actly

You need to find a route that picks up exactly 12 eggs to put in this carton. No yolking!

Start

EGGS

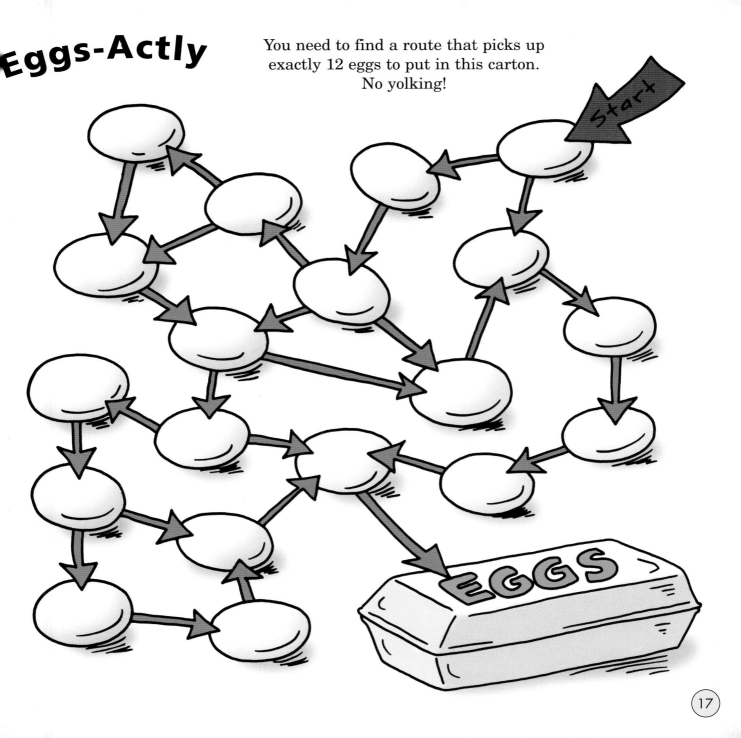

# Follow the Yellow Bricks

start

That's right. Follow the yellow brick road through this maze!

End

# Heart to Heart

Plan this heartfelt journey carefully. Only one route
of arrows will get you to the end.

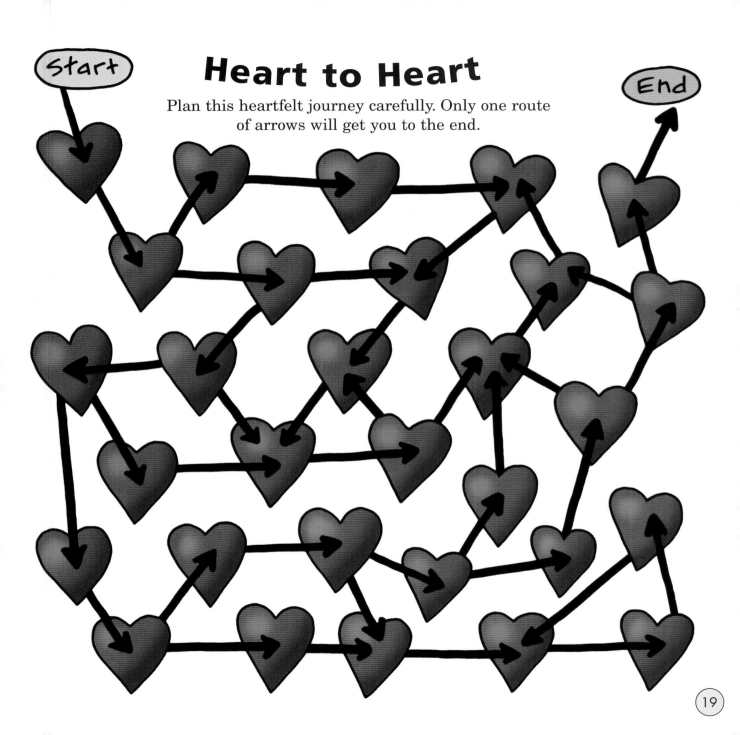

# Hedge **Your Bets**

Hedge mazes are some of the oldest mazes around, but lucky for you, your fingers can do the walking through this one.

# Inflation

You're going to have to pump your-self up to solve this one. Good luck! (You can follow hoses that pass under other hoses.)

# It's Soda Messy

What do you get when you put baking soda and vinegar together? A mess—and this maze!

start

End!

# Leap Frog

Help this frog leap across these lily pads to join his friend for a nice lunch of dried flies. Follow the arrows to find the correct route.

Start

End

Flies

# Liquid Metal

Mercury is the only metal that is liquid at room temperature. What route could you use to tilt this box so that mercury travels from the upper left corner to the lower right?

# Listen Up

Which plug leads to which noisy appliance? (You can follow cords that go under other cords.)

Start

25

# Looking Mighty Vine

And what a might vine this is! Can you find the way from the ground to the melon? (You can follow vines that pass under other vines.)

# Map It Out

John and Joan are planning a trip from Oak City to Tucker. How can they get there and visit *every* city on the map *exactly once*?

# Measure Up

You'll have to inch your way through the
tangle of tape measures in this yard.
Solving it would be quite a feet!

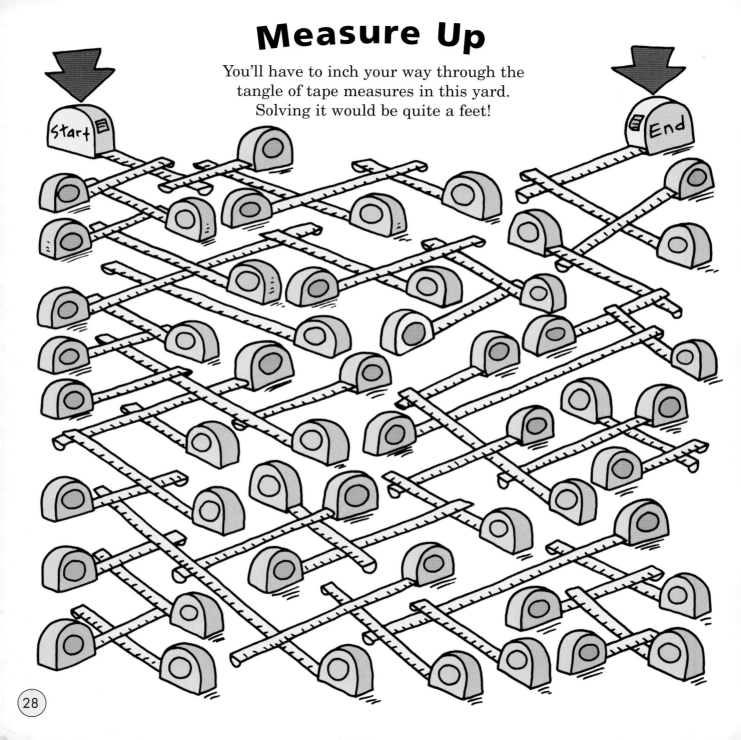

# Molehill

This mole has made a mountain of a molehill. Can you help him get to it?

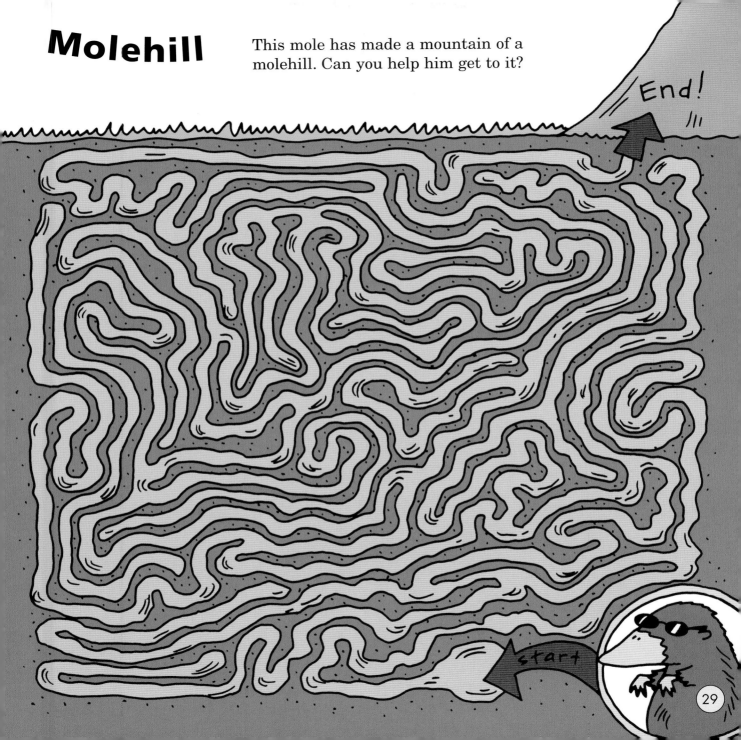

End!

start

# O! What a Mess!

O! Spilled cereal! What's next—spilled milk? And what will be cried then?

# Petal Picking

One animal has picked one petal, one has picked two, and the last has picked three. Can you figure out which animal did which picking?

# Road Crossing

How did the chicken cross the road?
Follow the tracks to find out.

start

End

# Safety First

Can you pin down the correct route through this tangle?

Start

End

# Slide Rule

Down, down, down you'll have to go
to get through this maze.

Start

End

# Slips Up

Follow the symbols to get from "Start" to "End." The first slip shows you how.

# Soak a Cola

I guess this is one way to reduce the number of calories in a can of cola. Unfortunately, it greatly increases the number of calories on the floor.

# Step on It

What's afoot? The prince was just here and left his prints. Can you prance through them to the end?

Start

End

38

# Stick with It

We couldn't finish this book without squeezing in a glue maze—and here it is!

Start

# Target Hopping

So many targets, so little time. Can you get through this one in less than a minute?

Start

End

# Telephone Tag

School has been cancelled—but Will doesn't know it yet! Jim can call either Bob or Brenda. Each of them can only call two others, and so on. Can you find the route that will wake up Will . . . so that he can then go back to sleep?

# Tiddlywinks

Forty winks is a nap. Not many people know it, but 40 winks are also 10 tiddlywinks. If you can find a route that passes through each of the 10 large, red tiddlywinks exactly once, you can take a nap.

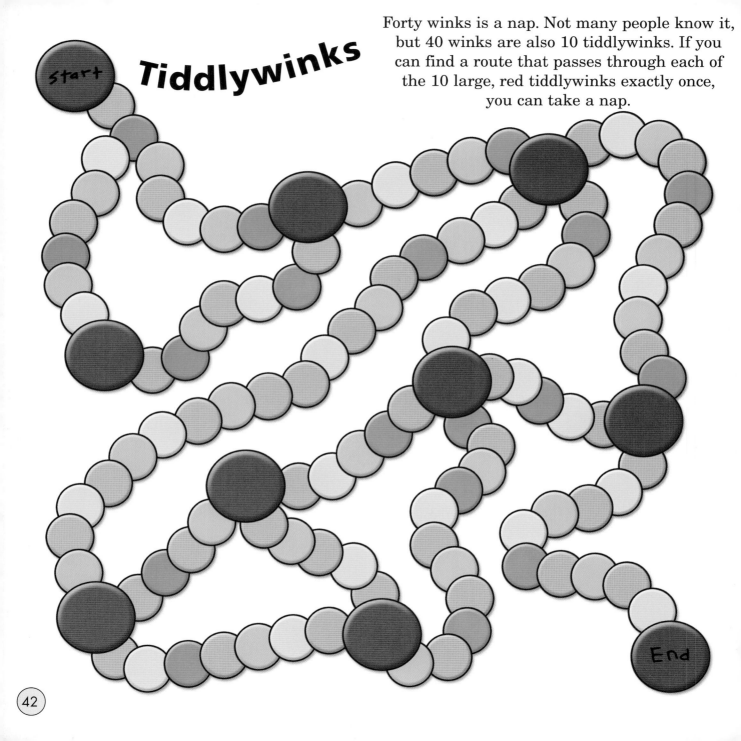

Start

End

# Walkway

This is the last maze, but no need to walk away disappointed. With this walkway maze, you can walk away doing a really fun maze. What better way to go!

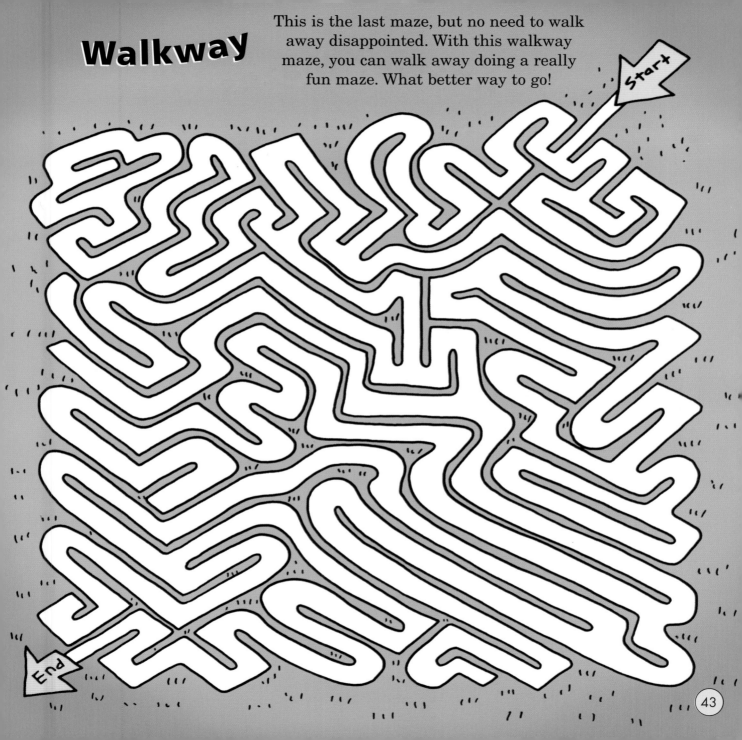

# Answer Mazes

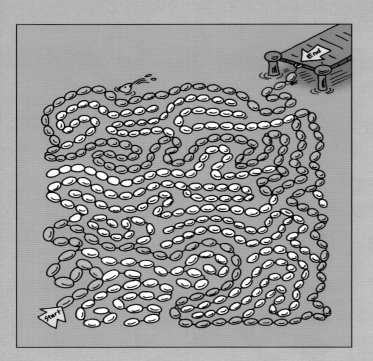

**Atta Buoy!**

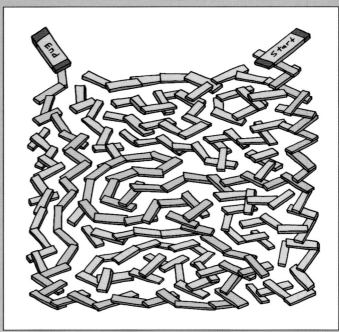

**Bar Made**

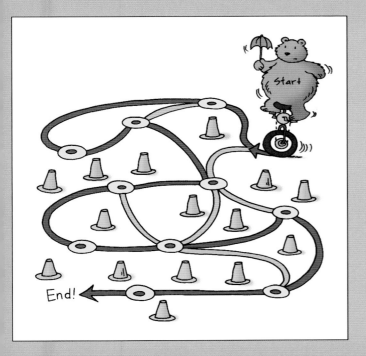

**Bear With It**

**Brush Up**

**Can You Dig It?**

**Crayon Playing**

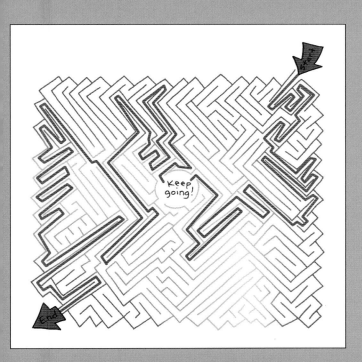

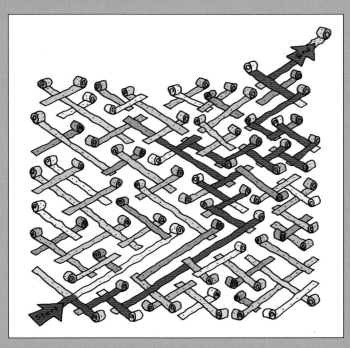

**Crazy Mazy**

**Crepe Race**

**Crowing Time**

**Delta Journey**

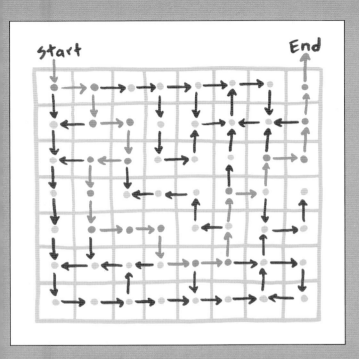

**Dot to Dot**

**Drawing the Line**

49

**Easel Does It**

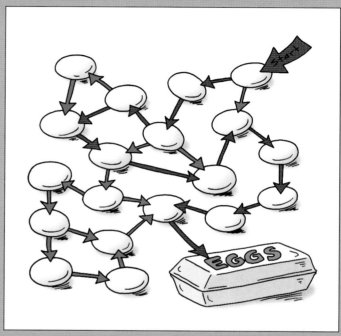

**Eggs-Actly**

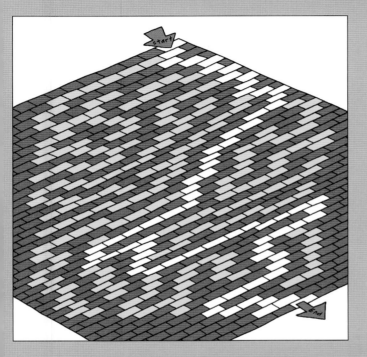

**Follow the Yellow Bricks**

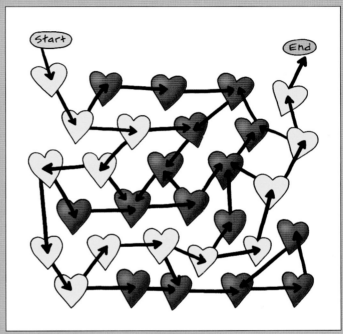

**Heart to Heart**

**Hedge Your Bets**

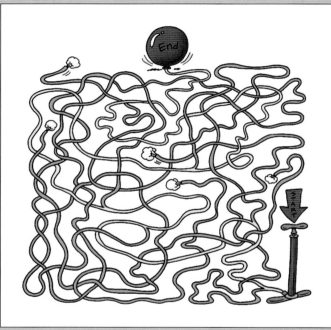

**Inflation**

**It's Soda Messy**

**Leap Frog**

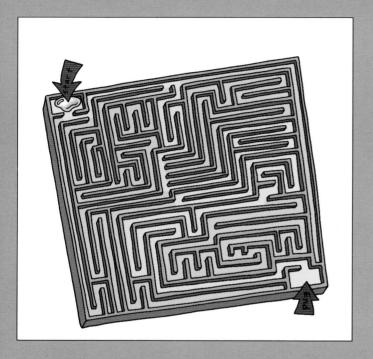

**Liquid Metal**

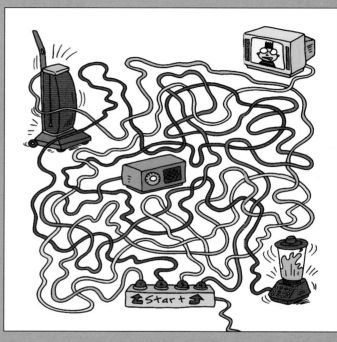

**Listen Up**

**Looking Mighty Vine**

**Map It Out**

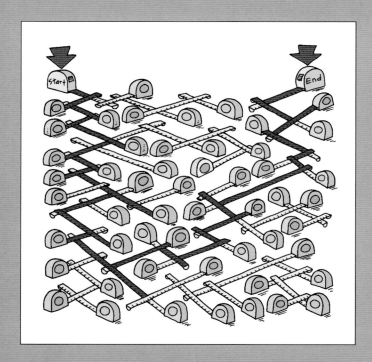

**Measure Up**

**Molehill**

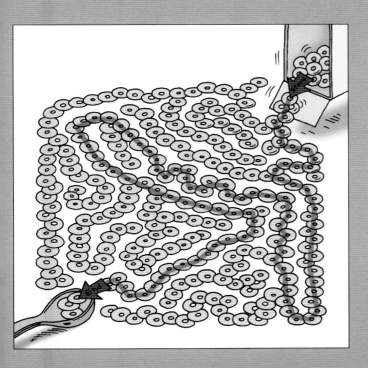

**O! What a Mess!**

**Petal Picking**

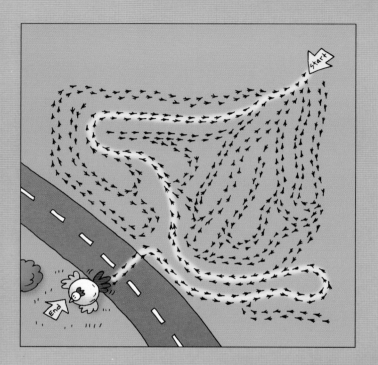

**Road Crossing**

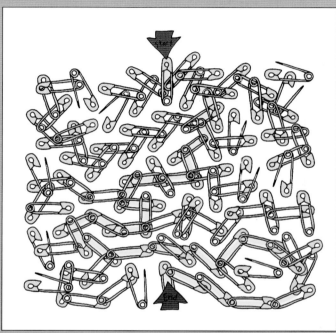

**Safety First**

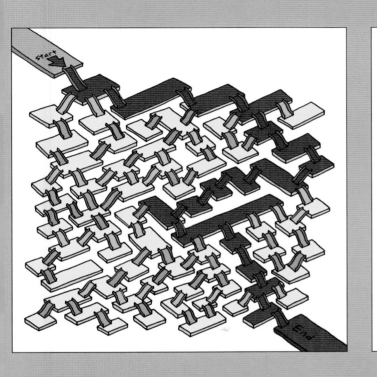

**Slide Rule**

**Slips Up**

**Soak a Cola**

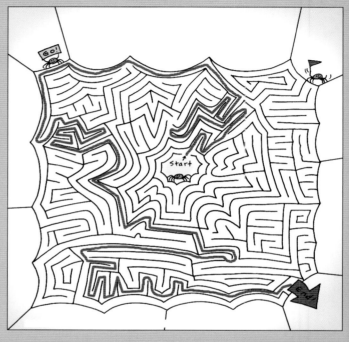

**Spider-Lympics**

**Step on It**

**Stick with It**

**Target Hopping**

**Telephone Tag**

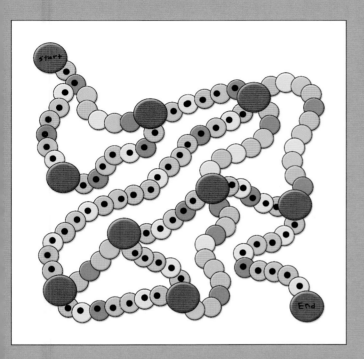

**Tiddlywinks**

**Walkway**

# Index

Pages in **bold** refer to solutions